LOVE IS

Marvin Heiferman   Carole Kismaric

A Lookout Book
powerHouse Books, New York

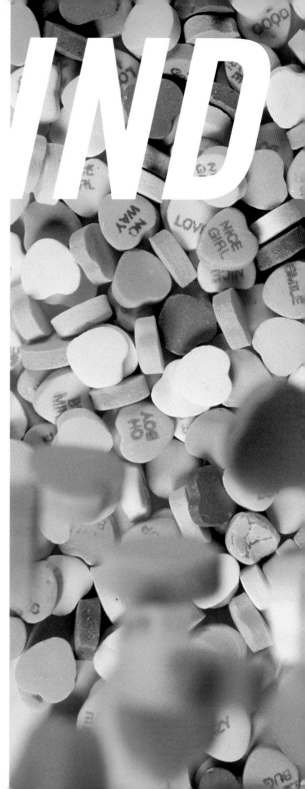

Love Is Blind is the self-help book for anyone who's ever been in love or wanted to be. It's a love song in pictures for all of us who are in love, who search for love, who yearn for love, who'll do anything to stay loved. It's a perfect valentine for anyone who's given up, too tired to fight in the war zone of love.

Love Is Blind maps love across America today: the peaks and valleys, the deserts and rivers, the superhighways and dead ends. It's a true-false test, a chance to measure our private love experiences against the demonstrations of love we see around us every day. If you recognize yourself in any of these pictures—wishing for love, empowered by love, dependent on love, a victim of love, shopping for a substitute when love isn't around—smile, and realize how convoluted love is and how vulnerable we are to love's call.

Because what we need and expect from love is often different from what we get, we're targets for anyone or anything pitching a love connection: the product that makes you more lovable, if you

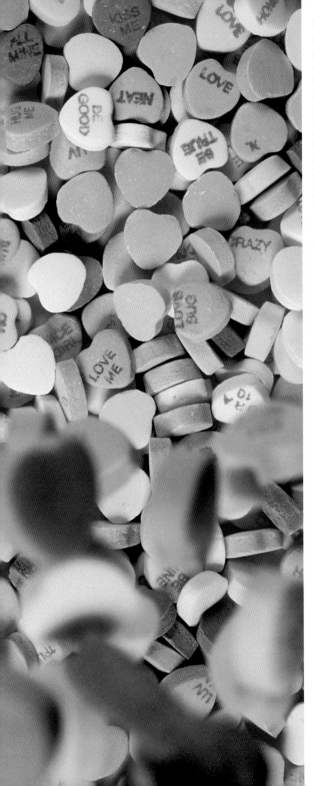

buy it; the fantasy that comes true, if you have the nerve to act it out; the god who loves you unconditionally, if you believe; the idol who arouses your passions, once you submit. From the mother's breast we grab to the body parts we squeeze to the hand we reach for when we die, looking for love is a full-time preoccupation and a lifelong engagement. Each of us discovers, in our own way, whether we're open or closed to love, how we cope with love when we have it, and how we react when love grows, changes, or fades.

Love brings out the best in us, and sometimes the worst. Still, we keep trying, falling in love, looking for love, wishing for love—be it romantic, narcissistic, forbidden, mis-placed, obsessive. No matter where you stand on the subject—for better and for worse, for richer or poorer— take a look and have a laugh. See why love—that many splendored thing—makes the world go round.

Yorker, Glamour, Vogue, Playboy, Vanity Fair and Ayn Rand. I'm somewhat handicapped, usually the slowest swimmer in the pool. You're fit and feminine, 25-40. You look forward to revealing your soul, mind and body to me. You like attracting men's attention in public, baring your pretty skin, muscles and curves with skimpy shorts and backless dresses. I'm especially excited by taller, smaller breasted women going braless. Meeting men is easy, but you want more conversation and commitment. We'll talk and touch, eat and sleep together. You like your work, but you'll stay home when we have kids. I'm usually kind and gentle, but my wicked, erotic impulse is to spank you! Guardian Box #1194F (exp.04/12)

Your Fantasy

You are in your 20's, attractive and sexy. You want a rendezvous... twice a week or so. Safe but alluring. I'm a normal, financially comfortable guy with healthy appetites, a stable guy who wants a discreet, wild, possibly longterm relationship to live out my fantasies in a safe way. Affable, nice-looking. Tall blonde or redhead preferred, but any normal, really pretty, sensuous, agreeable WF. No drugs. Go ahead and make the first sultry move. #1213 (exp.04/12).

scuba, silly playful dress up. Mid-Peninsula.   #1169 (exp.04/05).

Erotically assertive educator, understanding divorced WM, 54, desiring bright, feminine, sexually submisssive, sweetheart, 36-48. Goal: Enduring, passionate, affectionate, safe relationship. Novice welcomed. 4104 24th Street #129, S.F. 94114. #1182 (exp.04/19).

Talk To Me

Boy, 26, loves to talk dirty to older women. #1157 (exp.04/05).

Hot Master

Experienced and handsome master (30) has positions(!) available for novice to intermediate submissive female, 18-35. Firm tenderness and mutual enjoyment are primary.   Curious?   #1177 (exp.04/05).

Submissive Wanted

Single WM, 36, 5'10", looking for a young submissive to discipline and teach. I love ice cubes, blindfolds, toys and hot tubs. #1176 (exp.04/05).

Devastating in catsuit, molded figure, extremely feminine, exotic all around from head to toe. Asian transvestite searching educated, muscular, gorgeous single WM only, 25-35. #1223 (exp.04/12).

Straight Boy Wanted

GWM, 6'1", 180lbs., seeks straight (or bi) men who want to lay back and be serviced.

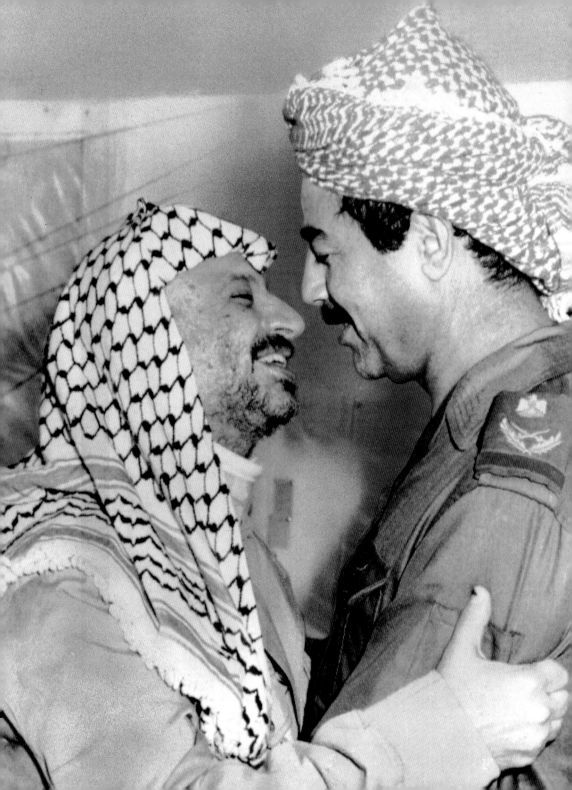

KISS MY FACE

M O I S T U R E
B A T H

R O M A N C E
B A T H

FOAMING BATH & SHOWER GEL

16 FL. OZ. (473ml)

FACE ON NEPTUNE

Voyager 2 photos just like the ones on Mars & Venus!

WEEKLY WORLD NEWS

September 19, 1989   30587   70¢

TALK WITH THE DEAD
America's No. 1 psychic tells you how to do it!

Hundreds in shopping mall watch in horror as . . .

KISSING COUPLE BURSTS INTO FLAMES!

'Their lips touched . . . . 30 seconds later they were ashes!'

Watch pounds fall off with amazing diet for autumn

★ ★ ★

Man trapped in a hedge — for 3 days!

YOU BE THE JUDGE!
What would you do to the fiends who murdered this little boy?

DIVORCE SHOCKER!
Sexy wife cheated on husband — with 137 men

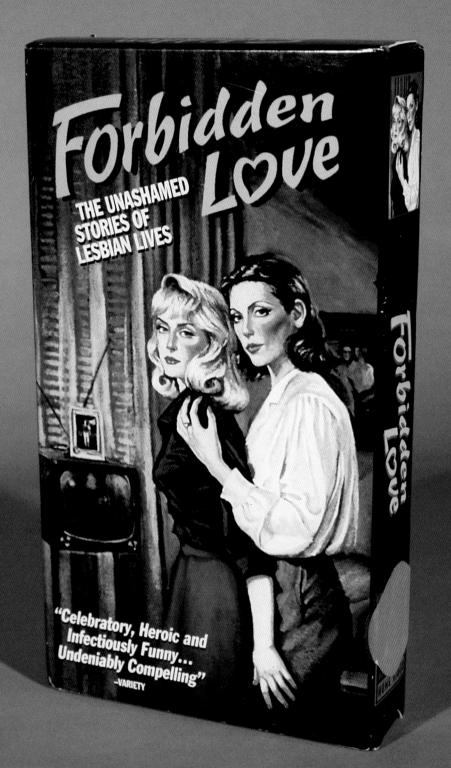

Pact: The Answer M... continued from p. 39

APRIL 1993

EVERYONE THINKS I MURDERED MY HUSBAND!

JUNE 1994

Modern Romances

$1.69 USA
$1.99 Canada

MY BOYFRIEND WANTS TO PAY ME FOR SEX

No Child Is Safe

MY LITTLE GIRL WAS KIDNAPPED IN OUR YARD!

HE RAPED ME— NOW, HE'S AFTER MY MOM

A Tearful Mother's Confession:

I HELPED MY SON KILL HIMSELF!

I HAD TO SNEAK INTO MY OWN DAUGHTER'S WEDDING

MACFADDEN WOMEN'S GROUP
WPS 35184

he held a knife to her stomach
threatening to cut out their unborn
child. Charly says she made the
right decision not to marry Doug

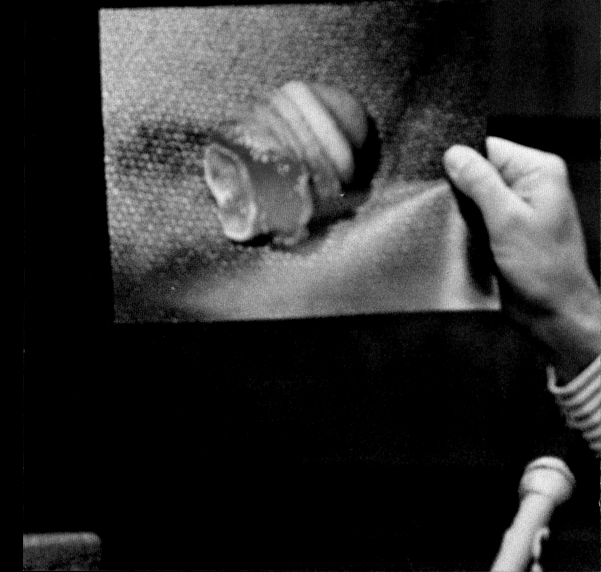

O · JERRY L NOLAND · BILLY RA
· ROLAND A PROVENCAL · RC
LUCAS · WALTER J SALLEY · EDV
D Jr · JEFFREY O LYNE · EARL K
DANIEL S BRITTAIN · GARY A HA
LLINGSWORTH · CARL D VIOLA
O · JOHN R RIDDLE · THOMAS
IAM R EDMONDSON · JAMES
H · NED R HERROLD · RONALD
· LEWIS C ROLLINS · ARMON
· GERALD W BAYLES · MICHA
NK A RAZO · PETER F SCHRAM
UR BROXTON Jr · DELBERT L
S O GILBERT ·

...LD MARK · RICARDO L M...
PATRICK · ERNEST G PAUL ·
...ALD RALICH · ROY J RICHAR...
...RD C SEXTON · WALTER B S...
...NES · CHARLES E WALKER ·
...NOTT · FRANCOIS J BUILAER...
...KEVIN M FLAHERTY · ROSS A...
...OLLINS · BOBBY JOE ALBER...
...AY · DONALD C GREEN ·
...KINSKY · LEONARD J KROSH...
...SHINGLEDECKER + MARTIN...
...D BURT · EDWARD S KOPIK...
...JOSEPH W SCHUSTER ·
...N · MIGUEL CASTRO G...

NO FAULT DIVORCE

- IN -

7 DAYS

- BY -

MUTUAL CONSENT

- ONLY -

LEGAL & PRIVATE

DIVORCE COUNSELORS, INC.

215 DA 9-9381

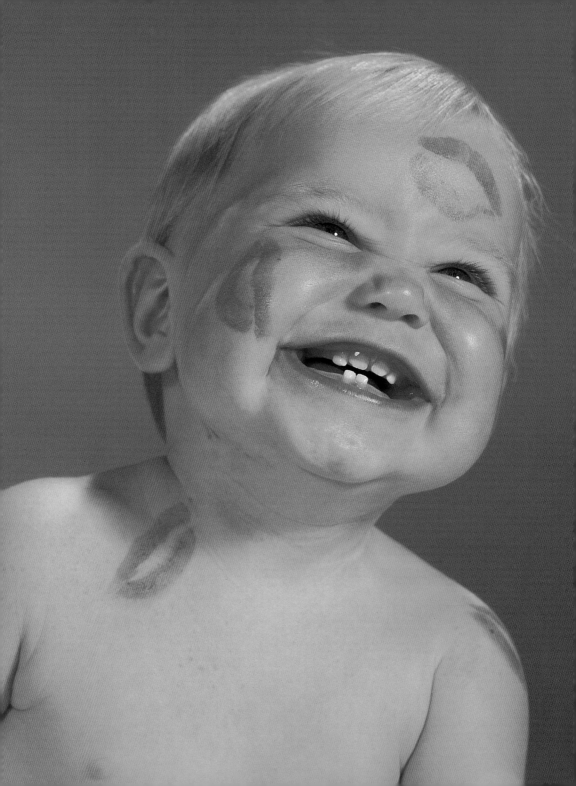

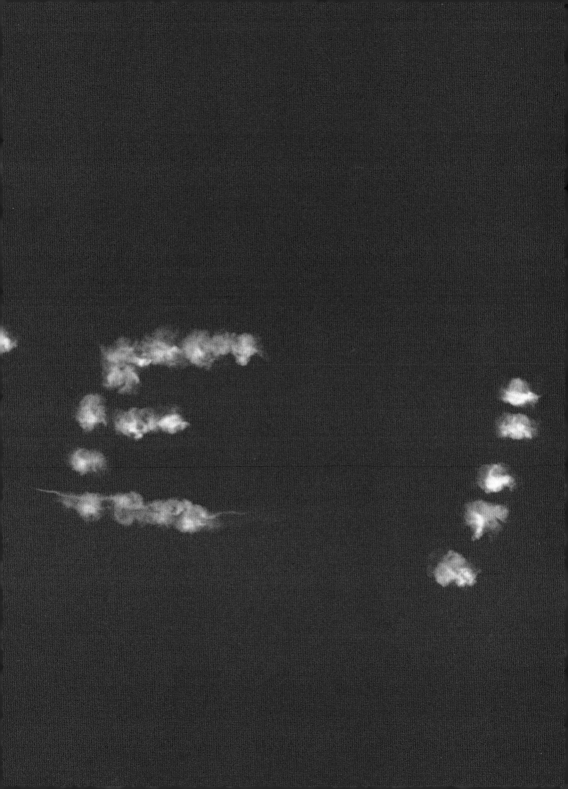

Dedicated to Allan Chasanoff, whose love of pictures and faith in us has made us feel loved.

Acknowledgments

Thanks to Daniel Power and Paula Curtz of powerHouse Books, who made this book happen, Chip Kidd and Elizabeth Ellis for their talent and good spirit, Alanna Stang for keeping the book's heart beating, Kate Lacey for her pictures and Ramia Mazé for all-around help. It's only with the love and help of our friends at picture agencies—especially Roberta Groves, Michael Shulman, Jocelyn Clapp, Ron and Howard Mandelbaum, Cristine Argyrakis—that this book could have been completed. Thanks also to Sid Avery, Bonni Benrubi, Douglas Blau, Jessica Brackman, Michael Friend, Charles Gatewood, Meryl Holland, Peter C. Jones, Pierce Rafferty, Michael Read. Without the love of Maurice Berger and András Szántó we'd have been lost.

Photo Credits

Archive Photos: 25, 32, 34, 37, 42, 45, 50-51, 53, 58, 61, 62, 63, 76; Ralph Bartholomew Jr. courtesy Keith De Lellis: 11; The Bettmann Archive: 10, 15, 19, 24, 28, 30, 31, 38-39, 40, 41, 52, 64, 66, 67, 69, 73, 82, 87; Caesars Pocono Resorts: The Cleopatra Suite featuring world-famous, patented seven-foot-high Champagne Glass Whirlpool Bath, patent number 294,290: 44; Eileen Cowin: 1; Ewing Galloway/American Stock Photography: 16, 74; FPG International: cover (Dennis Hallinan), 8 (Laszlo Willinger), 23, 33, 56-57, 65, 71, 72, 83, 84; Fernand Fonssagrives: 70; Richard Gordon: 48; Ernst Haas Studio: 94-95; H. Armstrong Roberts: 7, 12, 18, 68, 75, 86, 89; Collection of Marvin Heiferman: 91, 92; Heinz Pet Products: 29; Abigail Heyman: 78-79; Kate Lacey: 4-5, 6, 13, 14, 17, 20, 29, 43, 47, 60, 85; Magnum Photos: 55 (Eve Arnold); Frank Majore: 90; Petrified Collection/The Image Bank: 2-3; Photofest: 9, 21, 22, 26-27, 35, 36, 46, 54, 59, 77, 88; Joyce Ravid: back cover; Reckitt & Colman: 85; Sharon Smith: 93; Weekly World News: 14; Women Make Movies: 17; World Wide Photos/AP, New York: 49, 80-81.

Published in the United States by powerHouse Books

powerHouse Books is a division of powerHouse Cultural Entertainment, Inc.
635 East Ninth Street, #19, New York, New York 10009-4705, telephone 212-982-3154, fax 212-982-2171

A Lookout Book
1024 Avenue of the Americas, New York, New York 10018, telephone 212-221-6463, fax 212-719-0377

First edition, 1996
Library of Congress Cataloging-in-Publication Data:
Love is blind / [compiled by] Marvin Heiferman, Carole Kismaric. --
1st ed.
    p.   cm.
    "A Lookout book."
    ISBN 1-57687-007-3
    1. Love--Pictorial works. I. Heiferman, Marvin. II. Kismaric,
Carole, 1942- .
BF575.L8L67 1996   96-30552
306.7--dc20   CIP
            ISBN 1-57687-007-3

Distribution in the United States and Canada by D.A.P./Distributed Art Publishers
telephone 800-338-BOOK, fax 908-363-0338
10 9 8 7 6 5 4 3 2 1
Printed in Hong Kong

Cover Design by Chip Kidd
Production by Elizabeth Ellis